# The Case of the Dead Batsman

*Peter Viney*

G Garnet
Oracle

Garnet
EDUCATION

**Peter Viney** – author of this book, and Series Editor of the Garnet Oracle Readers – has over 40 years' experience teaching English and writing ELT materials. He now combines his writing with lecturing and teacher-training commitments internationally. He has authored and co-authored many successful textbook series and developed a wide range of highly popular video courses. Peter has been series editor and author on a number of graded reader series, and has also published with Garnet Education the highly popular *Fast Track to Reading*.

**Published by**
Garnet Publishing Ltd.
8 Southern Court
South Street
Reading RG1 4QS, UK

www.garneteducation.com

Copyright © Garnet Publishing Ltd 2013

ISBN 978 1 90757 521 1

First published 2014.
Reprinted 2015.

British Cataloguing-in-Publication Data
A catalogue record for this book is available from the British Library.

**Production**
Series editor:           Peter Viney
Project management:      Nicky Platt
Design and layout:       Mike Hinks
Illustration:            Kay Dixey

**Printed and bound** in Lebanon by
International Press: interpress@int-press.com

# 1 Elementary, my dear Watson

It was a warm, sunny July day during the summer of 1889. That morning I had received a letter from *The Strand Magazine*. They had been pleased with my stories about my old friend, Sherlock Holmes, and so they wanted to know if I had any more stories about his detective work. The summer is rarely a busy time for doctors, and I had not seen Holmes for some time. I decided to visit him in his rooms at Baker Street.

I walked slowly along Baker Street. I was enjoying the sunshine and thinking about some of the strange cases that Holmes had investigated. I heard the sound of the violin just before I reached number 221b. It was an interesting sign. Holmes always played his violin when he was thinking about a mystery, or a difficult case. I knocked on the door, and was taken to his rooms by his landlady, Mrs Hudson. Holmes answered the door immediately.

'Ah, Watson,' he said. 'Come in, come in. I knew it was you.'

I walked into the room and coughed. My eyes hurt too. The room was full of smoke. Holmes always smoked his pipe when he was worried. And as usual, all the windows were closed.

'That pipe will kill you, Holmes!' I said. 'You must know that.'

'You say that every time, Watson,' he said.

'Because it's true. I *am* a doctor, Holmes. May I open the window?'

Holmes nodded. I opened the window and let in some fresh air. I breathed deeply. Holmes coughed several times.

'I hate fresh air, Watson!' he said.

'Anyway, how are you?' I asked. 'And how did you know it was me at the door?'

'Elementary, my dear Watson, elementary,' he replied. 'First, I heard your footsteps on the stairs. I always know your footsteps, because you walk with a limp. You have limped since you were injured in the army nine years ago. A bullet hit you in the knee, and your left leg is shorter than your right leg. Secondly, you arrived on foot. I did not hear the sound of a horse and carriage outside. You have always enjoyed walking in the sunshine, and it is a very hot day. Most people would travel in a carriage on a day like this. Thirdly, just before I opened the door, I could smell coffee. I know you always drink strong black coffee in the morning.'

Holmes put his nose next to my jacket and breathed in. 'It was Jamaican Blue Mountain coffee this morning,' he said. 'You chose well. And finally, I heard my landlady talking to you on the stairs. She said, "Come this way, Dr Watson." It's very simple.'

I laughed. Holmes had always enjoyed playing little tricks on me. He picked up his violin from the chair.

'Sit down, my dear fellow,' he said. 'I promise that I shan't play the violin while you are here.'

'Ah, the violin,' I said. 'You usually play the violin when you have a problem. Are you working on a case at the moment?'

'Well done, Watson!' he replied. 'You'll be a detective yourself one day. Yes, in fact I'm working on one of the strangest cases I've ever seen.'

'You mean it's stranger than the case of the Queen of Ruritania's diamond jewellery?'

'Ah, yes!' said Holmes, 'I read what you wrote about that case in *The Strand Magazine*. You were very kind about my investigation. No, this case is stranger, and more dangerous too, I believe. Have you been reading the sports pages in the newspaper recently?'

'The sports pages? Well, no, I haven't. It's July and all the news is about cricket. I'm not interested in cricket, as you know. I prefer rugby football. I played rugby football at school, and when I was in the army in India, and …'

'Yes, of course, of course,' said Holmes. 'You have often told me. But perhaps you should read this.'

Holmes gave me a copy of *The Morning News*, and pointed to a story on the last page. I started to read it.

# 2 From *The Morning News*

## SECOND TRAGIC ACCIDENT IN VILLAGE CRICKET MATCH

Havelock, Devon. On Sunday afternoon, Mr Giles Pendryth was killed during a cricket match between two village teams, Havelock and Falmoor. Mr Pendryth, a popular local farmer, was playing for the Havelock team. He was batting when he was struck on the forehead by the cricket ball. Mr Pendryth was killed at once.

The accident is a terrible coincidence. Two weeks ago, another member of the Havelock team, Mr James Dodds, was hit on the forehead by a cricket ball during a match between Havelock and Dartpuddle. He was taken to the nearest hospital in Exeter, where he died three hours later.

Mr Pendryth, who lived at Westmoor Farm just outside Havelock, leaves a young widow, Mrs Juliet Pendryth. They were married only four weeks ago. Mr Frederick Truebody, the Falmoor player who threw the ball which killed Mr Pendryth, was badly shocked by the accident, and says he will never play cricket again.

'Why, Holmes!' I said. 'What a terrible and tragic story. How sad! Think of his poor young wife. I had no idea that cricket was so dangerous!'

'It usually isn't,' Holmes replied.

'It isn't? But two men have died in one village cricket team in only two weeks. If you don't call that dangerous, then …'

'I have been investigating cricket matches, Watson,' said Holmes. 'In the last twenty-five years, three people have been killed during cricket matches. Two of them were Pendryth and Dodds during the last two weeks, in the same village cricket team.'

'What a tragic coincidence!' I said.

'Coincidence, Watson? Or perhaps it's something more than a coincidence.'

'But Holmes, surely cricket is quite dangerous. I mean the ball is small, and heavy, and very hard. And when a good player throws it, the ball moves very fast.'

'Bowl.'

'Pardon?'

'The word is *bowl*, Watson. In cricket, the man who "throws" the ball is the bowler. And so he doesn't "throw" it. He bowls it.'

'I know that, Holmes! I had to play cricket at school. I'm not completely stupid. I said "throw", but I meant …'

'Yes,' said Holmes, 'it's not important. A fast bowler can bowl … or "throw" if you prefer … the ball at about ninety miles an hour. The distance from the bowler to the batsman is exactly twenty-two yards. There is little time to move out of the way. But accidents rarely happen because the bowler does not throw the ball at the batsman. He is trying to hit the wicket, which is behind the batsman. The wicket is those three pieces of wood which …'

'Very funny, Holmes,' I replied. 'I know what a wicket is. But accidents can happen in any sport.'

'Of course. But it is very strange. How did the ball hit them both on the forehead? A ball which hit you on the arm, or shoulder, or face, would injure you seriously. But a ball on the forehead is needed to kill a man. Am I correct, *Doctor* Watson?'

'Well, yes, I'm sure you're right. But it's so tragic. This fellow Pendryth had only been married for a short time.'

'Murder is always tragic, Watson.'

'Murder? But how? Why?'

Holmes smiled. 'What are you doing tomorrow, Watson?'

'Nothing important,' I said.

'Very well, then. Would you like to come to Devon with me? I shall be there for two days ... no longer.'

'Yes, yes, of course. I can ask Dr Harris to help me. He can look after my patients. But why ...?'

'Do you remember Colonel Abbot, Watson? We met him when I was investigating the case of the private diary which was stolen from the Prince of Wales.'

'Colonel Abbot? Yes, he was working for the Prince. Nice fellow.'

'He left the army two years ago and moved to Havelock. His family home is in Havelock. He was born there. He sent me a telegram this morning, asking for my help. Look, here it is. I replied immediately. We're catching the 7.15 train in the morning. I'll meet you at Paddington Station, Platform Four. And don't forget your notebook, Watson. I think you may have another story quite soon.'

# POST OFFICE TELEGRAM

| office stamp | |
| --- | --- |
| HAVELOCK, DEVONSHIRE | **POST OFFICE** |
| 9th JUL 1889 | **TELEGRAPHS.** |
| Handed in at | |
| Havelock | |

Office of origin and service instructions

SHERLOCK HOLMES, ESQ. 221B BAKER STREET,
LONDON NW

HOLMES. HAVELOCK BATSMEN STORY. NEED YOUR HELP.
PLEASE COME AS SOON AS POSSIBLE. COL. ABBOT.

words 15

received London NW office: 7.56 a.m.

I stood up and moved towards the door. 'I have to walk past Paddington Station this afternoon. Shall I get the tickets? We might be in a hurry tomorrow.'

'There's no need, Watson,' said Holmes. 'I've already bought them.'

I stopped. 'But how did you know I could come to Devon?'

Holmes smiled, 'I know you, Watson. You would not miss a story like this.'

# 3 The 7.15 to Devon

When I reached the platform the next morning, it was already thirteen minutes past seven. Holmes had boarded the train. He was standing by the door and waving at me through the open window. I hurried along the platform and climbed onto the train, just as it began moving.

'My dear Watson,' he said, 'do sit down. You've been running. I'm sorry that you had to eat your breakfast so quickly. I see that you still have two eggs for your breakfast, with half a tomato and black coffee.'

I was surprised, 'But Holmes, how did you know what I had for breakfast?'

'It's simple, Watson. An elementary problem. I know that you ate quickly, and that you had eggs, tomato and coffee. There is a little egg on your shirt, a little piece of tomato on your moustache, and a small coffee stain on your jacket. You are normally a very careful man, and so I know that you were in a hurry.'

'In a hurry? I certainly was. I had to visit a patient at half past midnight. I didn't go to sleep until two. That's the reason I woke up late. I had to hurry. I didn't have time to buy a newspaper!'

'I've bought one for you,' said Holmes. 'Here it is.'

We sat down and read our newspapers, and the journey passed pleasantly. We left the train at Exeter, and after a short wait we boarded the local train to Havelock. Holmes was looking out of the window.

'We're travelling at just over fifty miles an hour,' he said. 'That's very fast for a local train.'

'Really?' I said. 'My dear Holmes, how do you know?'

'It's quite elementary, Watson,' he replied. 'There are exactly sixty yards between each of the telegraph poles along the Great Western Railway. You can calculate the speed of the train from that. Just count the time between the poles.'

I looked out of the window and tried to calculate the speed. I couldn't do it. I tried with a pen and paper. I still couldn't do it.

After a short journey, the train arrived at Havelock Station. Holmes and I climbed down onto the platform. I recognized the tall man with white hair and a white moustache who was waiting for us on the platform.

'Colonel Abbot!' I said. 'It's very kind of you to come and meet us.'

'Dr Watson!' he said. 'It's good to see you again. And you, Mr Holmes, thank you for coming to help us.'

We shook hands and followed Colonel Abbot out to his carriage. He took us to his house, which was a beautiful eighteenth-century building in the centre of the village. Tea was brought at once, and we sat down.

Holmes spoke first. 'What do the police think about these two tragic deaths, Colonel Abbot?'

'I'm afraid our local policeman is not very clever,' he replied. 'He believes both deaths were accidents. But you see, Giles Pendryth was my nephew. He was my dear sister's son, and she died ten years ago. So I've been like a father to him. And he's been like a son to me.'

'Your nephew?' I said. 'I didn't know. I'm very sorry.'

'Thank you,' said Colonel Abbot. 'Giles was the best cricketer in the village. He was a wonderful batsman. I was watching the match when he was killed ...' He looked at the floor for a moment, then breathed deeply. 'You see ... he suddenly seemed to turn and just walk into the ball. It was like a football player, when they head the ball. But this was a hard cricket ball. Poor fellow. He was dead before he hit the ground.'

'You don't mean ... that he killed himself?' I said.

'Of course not!' said Colonel Abbot angrily. 'My nephew had everything. A farm. A beautiful new wife. He was the happiest man in the village.'

'I'm sorry,' I said. 'I didn't mean to ...'

'That's all right, Doctor. I understand. You have to ask difficult questions when something like this happens.'

I looked at Holmes. He was sitting quietly. He hadn't said a word. He was watching us and listening.

Colonel Abbot continued, 'It wasn't the bowler's fault. He thinks it *was* his fault, poor fellow. He says he will never play cricket again.'

'But why do you think it happened?' I asked.

'It's strange,' said the Colonel, 'but I saw Giles that morning, the morning of the day that he died. He was worried, I could see that. He said that somebody wanted to buy his farm. They had offered him a lot of money, a lot more money than the farm was worth, in fact. He didn't want to sell. The farm has belonged to his family for two hundred years, and he loved it. He was offered so much money. But he refused the offer. He refused to sell the farm.'

'Did he tell you who wanted to buy it?' said Holmes.

'That was the strange thing. He said that he couldn't tell me. He had made a promise. He had promised to tell nobody who the buyer was. A few hours later he was dead.'

'What about his wife?' I added. 'Didn't he tell her?'

'No. Fortunately Juliet wasn't here when it happened. Her sister was visiting, and they had gone to Exeter on the train. They had left early in the morning. She knows nothing about the offer. I've asked her.'

'What about the other fellow?' I asked. 'The one who was killed two weeks ago. I can't remember his name …'

'James Dodds,' said Holmes softly.

'Yes, poor old Dodds,' replied the Colonel. 'I never liked him. But that's another strange coincidence. Dodds owned the next farm to Giles's farm.'

'Had anyone tried to buy it?' asked Holmes.

'I have no idea,' said Colonel Abbot. 'Dodds didn't speak to anybody about it. He was a very quiet man. He didn't have many friends. He was born on that farm, and he had lived there all his life. He didn't have a family. He wasn't married and his parents died several years ago. The farm will go to his aunt, and she's in her eighties. She'll have to sell it.'

'What about Giles's wife … I mean, widow? What will she do?' I asked.

'She won't stay here,' replied the Colonel. 'She's from London, poor girl. No, Juliet will return to London. There's nothing for her in Havelock. Just sad memories.'

Colonel Abbot stood up. 'I'm sorry,' he said, 'I haven't stopped talking. You must both be hungry after your journey. Would you like some lunch?'

# 4 Dr Lennon

We followed Colonel Abbot into the dining room. We sat down and had an excellent lunch. The housekeeper brought us fresh vegetable soup, followed by a very hot chicken curry with rice.

'This is an excellent curry, Colonel Abbot,' I said. 'I haven't had a curry like this since I left India.'

Colonel Abbot smiled. 'I knew you had been in the Indian Army, Dr Watson. I asked my housekeeper to prepare it for you.'

'Has she ever been to India?' I asked. 'You can't get curry like this in England.'

'No, she hasn't,' said the Colonel, 'but the important thing is the curry powder.'

Holmes coughed. 'It's very hot,' he said, and drank some water. 'Where do you get the curry powder?'

'Ah, that's my secret,' said Colonel Abbot. 'You see ...'

At that moment the doorbell rang. The Colonel stopped. 'Ah, this will be my neighbour, Dr Lennon. I was expecting him to call today.'

Colonel Abbot's housekeeper came in.

'Dr Lennon's here, sir,' she said. 'I told him that you had visitors, but he said he wanted to see you.'

'Of course,' said the Colonel. 'Please show him in. He can join us for coffee.'

Dr Lennon was a short, suntanned man in his early fifties. 'Good afternoon, Colonel. Good afternoon, gentlemen. I am sorry to disturb you.'

'You're not disturbing us at all,' said the Colonel. 'I'm very pleased to see you. May I introduce my old friends? This is Mr Holmes and Dr Watson. This is Dr Lennon.'

'How do you do?' we said.

'How do you do, Mr Holmes?' he replied. 'How do you do, Dr Watson?' We shook hands.

'Mr Holmes ... Dr Watson ... please excuse my question, but are you Sherlock Holmes, the famous detective?'

Holmes smiled and nodded.

'And Dr Watson,' continued Dr Lennon, 'I've read several of your stories about Mr Holmes in *The Strand Magazine*. Well, this is most exciting.'

'Yes,' said Holmes softly, 'you and Dr Watson will have much to talk about. You were both doctors with the Indian Army, after all. Watson was in the North-West of India, of course, so you probably never met.'

'No ...' said Dr Lennon, then stopped. 'How do you know that I was in the Indian Army, Mr Holmes? And that I wasn't in the North-West?'

'Elementary, my dear sir. You walk like a soldier, with a straight back. You speak like a soldier. Your dark suntan tells me that you lived in a hot country for many years, and the tie you are wearing has the colours of the Queen's South India Horse Soldiers.'

Dr Lennon put his hand to his tie, which was light green, pink and gold. He laughed. 'Thank you, Mr Holmes, for showing us your powers as a detective,' he said.

'No, thank you, Dr Lennon. Colonel Abbot was just going to tell us the secret of his wonderful curry. I am afraid I have already guessed. You give him the curry powder.'

'Yes,' said Dr Lennon in surprise. 'I have it sent to me from India four times a year.' He turned to the Colonel. 'I'm afraid I've come about tomorrow's match,' he said. 'We have only ten men. Young Carter can't play, and Jack Miller doesn't want to play.'

Lennon turned to us. 'Have you heard about our terrible accidents?' he asked.

Holmes nodded. 'Yes, Colonel Abbot told us about them just now, while we were having lunch. How tragic!'

'You hadn't read about them in the newspapers?' he said.

'No,' said Holmes, to my surprise. 'You see, I've just returned from Switzerland, and Dr Watson has been very busy with his patients recently.'

'Really?' said Dr Lennon. 'July is usually a quiet time for doctors. There aren't many coughs or colds around.'

'There are in London,' said Holmes. 'I think it's because of all the smoke from the factories. It's good to be here in the country with all this fresh air.'

I stared at Holmes. Fresh air! The man hated the stuff!

Lennon continued, 'Well, this is the reason I have disturbed your lunch. I'm the captain of the village cricket team. We're playing against Baskerton tomorrow afternoon. It's difficult to find a team.'

Colonel Abbot shook his head. 'I'm sorry, Lennon,' he said. 'You know about my heart problem. I can't play myself.' He turned to Holmes. 'I'm the umpire nowadays. That's why I was watching when poor Giles was killed ... I was just twenty yards away.'

'This is fortunate,' said Holmes. 'You are lucky, Dr Lennon, because Watson here loves cricket. He used to play for his school, and then for his university college.'

I stared at Holmes again. 'But Holmes, I'm not good at ...' I started to say.

'Now, now, my dear Watson,' he said, 'don't be so modest! I'm sure you'd love to play!'

'I'm not being modest,' I said, 'I'm sure I'm not good enough ...'

'This is wonderful news, Dr Watson,' Lennon said. 'Are you a batsman or a bowler?'

'I'm neither ...'

'I told you not to be modest, Watson,' said Holmes. 'He's an excellent batsman,' he continued. 'He was quite famous at university.'

'But I can't run fast ...' I looked at Dr Lennon. 'I have a limp. You see, I injured my knee during my time in India. A bullet hit me in the knee, and ...'

'Nonsense. You ran fast enough for the train this morning,' said Holmes.

'But I haven't played since ...'

Holmes kicked me hard under the table before I could finish.

'No,' he said, 'Watson hasn't played since early June.'

Actually, I was going to say that I hadn't played since I was at school.

'June 5th, wasn't it?' Holmes said. 'I remember it well. Watson scored seventy-five.'

I could feel my face. It was hot. Holmes smiled. 'That curry was very hot,' he said. 'Look at your face, Watson. It's bright red!'

'It's not the curry ...' I started to say.

'Perhaps you would like to practise with the team this evening?' said Lennon. 'Colonel Abbot will be coming. We need an umpire.'

'Er ... er ...' I didn't know what I should say.

'Yes, that's an excellent idea,' said Holmes. 'I want to walk around and explore your lovely village. You'll excuse me if I don't come to the practice myself?'

'Of course,' said Lennon. 'We'll see you both at six o'clock then, Dr Watson ... Colonel. Good afternoon.'

# 5 The cricket match begins

I did not see Holmes again that evening. Colonel Abbot and I went to the practice. All the players seemed nervous. There was Dr Lennon, two local farmers, several young men from the village, and Adrian Fitzroy, the son of Lord Fitzroy, who owned a house near the village. I was worried about my limp, but speed and age isn't too important in cricket matches between villages. You can find players of sixteen years old and players of sixty years old in the same team. The practice game was quiet. The bowlers bowled slowly and carefully. Everyone was afraid of another accident. To my surprise, I batted quite well, but it was easy to hit slow balls. Most of the team weren't much better than me.

The only first-class player was Herbert Crane, who owned a local farm. He was the Havelock wicketkeeper, and he had the most dangerous job in the team. I should explain. The wicketkeeper has to stay close behind the wicket. His job is to catch any balls that the batsman misses. Crane was a nice fellow, and we talked about his animals. He was most proud of his cows. They produced more milk than any other cows in Devon. Crane's farm produced milk, cream, butter and cheese. He was beginning to send his cheese to shops in Exeter and London, and it was quite famous.

'I've spent years on this,' he told me, 'and my cheese gets better every year. My wife sometimes complains about all the work. So do I, but the farm is our life. We love it here.'

~

I spent a pleasant evening with Colonel Abbot. We had dinner, and I told him stories about my years in India. He was very kind and listened carefully, and laughed in all the correct places. I went to bed early and slept well. I think it was the fresh Devon air.

~

When I came downstairs for breakfast, Holmes was waiting for me.

'Ah, good morning, Holmes,' I said. 'Lovely morning, isn't it? I hope you slept well.'

'Yes, yes,' he said. 'Did you enjoy the practice?' He didn't wait for my reply, but continued, 'I have to go to Okehampton this morning, but I shall be back for the cricket match. I'll see you then.'

'Haven't you had breakfast?' I asked.

'No time!' He hurried away.

I had breakfast with Colonel Abbot, and then spent the morning walking around the village with him. We stopped at the village church. Giles Pendryth was buried there. There were fresh flowers. Colonel Abbot added some more.

'Juliet,' he said. 'She puts new flowers here every day. He was so young. She's too young to be a widow.' He turned away.

After lunch we went to the cricket field. It was a lovely, sunny afternoon with a clear blue sky, and the field looked beautiful. There were trees all around it, and there was a small white-painted cricket pavilion with two changing rooms (one for each team), a veranda and a small tea room. The Baskerton team had arrived early. Baskerton is only a few miles from Havelock, and all the players knew each other.

Holmes arrived a few minutes before the match started. He sat on the veranda with his pipe, with smoke all around him. I coughed. 'Holmes, you really shouldn't smoke here,' I said.

'Ah, yes. You're probably right, Watson. But I haven't brought my violin, and I have to think. Fresh air doesn't help me.'

The idea of Holmes playing his violin at a match made me laugh.

'Holmes,' I said, 'did you discover anything? Where did you go?'

'Not now, my dear Watson,' he replied. 'We shall know all the answers quite soon.'

'But ...'

'And another thing, old fellow,' he said. 'If I say anything that you don't understand, just agree with me.'

'But …'

'We'll talk about it later,' he finished.

Havelock batted first, or as cricketers say, Havelock had the first 'innings'. I felt that the Havelock batsmen were very nervous, and also that the Baskerton bowlers were not bowling as fast as they could. I sat on the veranda with the other Havelock players. I was the last batsman. Unfortunately, I was 'out' with the first ball. I missed it and it hit the wicket. Our team had scored 107, which was rather good, I thought. We all went in for tea and sandwiches before Baskerton had their innings.

During tea, I was talking to Adrian Fitzroy. He was a nice young fellow. He had just finished studying at my old college at the University of London, and I was telling him all about my time there. He was listening carefully, and enjoying my old stories. I noticed that Holmes was talking quietly to Colonel Abbot, who had been umpiring the match. Holmes came over to me. 'Have you seen Dr Lennon?' he asked.

'He's in the changing room,' said young Fitzroy. 'Herbert Crane was having a problem with his cricket boots. They're a new pair of boots. They were hurting his feet, and so he went to change into his old boots. Dr Lennon went with him to look at his feet.'

At that moment, Dr Lennon came into the tea room. He started talking to Mr Jones, the Baskerton umpire. Colonel Abbot walked towards them.

'Mr Jones,' said the Colonel, 'I am not feeling well. I have a heart problem, no, no, don't worry. It's nothing serious. But my friend, Dr Watson, has told me that I must not stay out in the hot sunshine. Fortunately, my friend Mr Holmes has offered to umpire for the rest of the match. Will that be all right?'

I could not believe my ears! As Colonel Abbot walked past me, he whispered, 'Sorry, Watson. Holmes asked me to say that.'

# 6 The match continues

After tea we walked out on to the field for the Baskerton innings. It certainly was hot out there, perhaps the hottest day of the year. The two Baskerton batsmen were tall, strong fellows. I was fielding, and Holmes was one of the umpires. The Havelock bowlers were still bowling slowly, and the batsmen had soon scored seventy. Several balls were hit past me and my knee was hurting badly when I tried to run after them. My limp was getting worse.

Dr Lennon, who was standing near me, called the bowlers to him. 'This is stupid,' he said. 'A third tragic accident is impossible. We have to bowl faster, or the match will be silly. These Baskerton fellows came here for a game of cricket, not to practise hitting slow balls around the field.'

'That's true,' said young Fitzroy. 'After all, our players were killed. We've never injured anyone from the other team. Our bowling isn't dangerous.'

'Exactly,' said Lennon. 'Fitzroy's quite right. So let's start trying!'

The Havelock players started bowling faster and harder, and soon one of the Baskerton batsmen was out. He hit a fast ball, it went behind the wicket, and Herbert Crane, our wicketkeeper, jumped up and caught the ball. It was a brilliant catch, and both teams congratulated him.

Fitzroy began bowling for Havelock, and he was a good, strong fast bowler. His second ball hit the wicket, and another Baskerton player was out. Crane congratulated him. 'Well done, Fitzroy,' he shouted. 'Keep bowling like that.'

I watched as Fitzroy ran to bowl the next ball. The batsman missed it. Herbert Crane caught the ball and threw it back to Fitzroy. Suddenly there was a flash of light in my eye and I couldn't see anything. It was like the sun coming from a mirror. I put my hand above my eyes so that I could see. Lennon was opposite me, a few yards away. The sun was shining on his pocket watch. I wondered why he was holding it.

'Come on, you fellows,' he called. 'It's nearly five o'clock! Let's start bowling fast!'

Fitzroy nodded, and started running forward to bowl the next ball. Suddenly, Herbert Crane stood straight up behind the wicket, and at that moment Holmes charged forward and pushed him to the ground. The ball hit Crane's shoulder and he screamed. We all ran forward. Holmes stood up. 'This is a job for you, Watson. His shoulder is broken, I think.'

Fitzroy had run over to help. He was shaking. 'I didn't mean to ...' he started to say.

'It's not your fault,' said Holmes. 'It's fortunate that I was here. That ball was going to hit him on the forehead. That's why I pushed him.'

'But I bowled at the wicket ...' said Fitzroy.

'I know,' said Holmes.

I was looking at Crane. His eyes were looking straight into the sky. I moved my hand over them. They didn't move.

I put my hand on his chest. He was breathing.

'Holmes,' I said, 'there's something wrong with him. He's breathing, his eyes are open, but he isn't seeing anything. The ball hit his shoulder, not his head, so why ...'

'I think Dr Lennon can help us,' said Holmes. 'Fitzroy! Smith! Take Dr Lennon's arms. I don't want him going anywhere for the moment.'

~

The players stood around us in the centre of the field.

'What is the meaning of this?' shouted Lennon angrily. 'Let go of my arms!'

'Hold him,' said Holmes. 'Mr Jones, perhaps you could call the village policeman. His house is just next to the church in the village.'

'Are you going to explain?' asked young Fitzroy.

'Of course,' said Holmes. 'Lennon put a drug in Crane's tea, and then he hypnotised him. That happened in the changing room. Then Lennon told Crane to try and hit the fastest and hardest ball he could with his forehead. Did any of you see a flash of light from Lennon's watch? He shone that at Crane just before the ball. That was his sign. When Crane saw the light, he was hypnotised immediately.'

'I don't understand, Holmes,' I said. 'You can hypnotise people, but you can't make them hurt themselves. There have been many studies of hypnotists, and people will never hurt themselves.'

'Correct, Watson,' said Holmes. 'That is usually true. But there is one drug that makes it possible. It is a very rare drug, and it is only found in the south of India. I think we will find some of the drug in Dr Lennon's left-hand jacket pocket. Could you look for me, Fitzroy?'

Young Fitzroy reached into Lennon's pocket and pulled out a small, dark blue glass bottle.

'Thank you,' said Holmes. 'Please be careful with the bottle. The police will need it for the murder investigation.'

'But why, Holmes?' said Colonel Abbot. 'What reason did Lennon have?'

'Dr Lennon discovered some plans. They are going to build a new railway line to Okehampton. The line will go from Havelock, and will go along the valley to the west. The valley where Pendryth, Dodds and Crane had their farms.'

'But we knew nothing of any plans,' said Colonel Abbot.

'They were secret. The railway didn't want anyone to know yet. Dr Lennon discovered the plans, and decided to buy all the farms in the valley. Then he could sell them to the railway company. I believe he has friends in the railway company, which is why he knew. So Dr Lennon hypnotised Pendryth and Dodds, and murdered them. He probably hoped to buy Crane's land, but when he saw me here, he thought it was too dangerous, so he

didn't make an offer. He decided to kill Crane, but not when he was batting. He was going to do it while he was wicketkeeper.'

'But no one could believe *three* tragic deaths ...' I said.

'Yes,' said Holmes, 'no normal person could believe it was coincidence. But remember, Lennon is a murderer. So Lennon is not a normal person. He had already killed two. He believed he could kill three.'

Lennon was taken away by the police. That evening, we all returned to Colonel Abbot's house. Crane was awake, and feeling better, but he couldn't remember anything about the changing room. Holmes sat in a chair and explained the mystery.

'As Watson knows,' he began, 'I have always been interested in hypnotism. As soon as I met Lennon, I recognized his name. He wrote a short, but most interesting book on hypnotism several years ago. Colonel Abbot told us that Pendryth's farm was next to Dodds's farm. I went to Okehampton, where I discovered the railway's plans.'

'They told you about them, then,' I said.

'I said I discovered the plans, Watson,' said Holmes. 'I won't tell you how. Then I looked at some maps, and I knew at once that Herbert Crane was in danger. His farm was the next one along the valley. I decided to take Colonel Abbot's job as umpire. In that way, I could stand near Mr Crane.'

'You were sure it was Lennon?' said Colonel Abbot. 'Why?'

'That was easy,' said Holmes. 'I looked at the army records for the last twenty years. Colonel Abbot has a copy over there. He has all the records of army officers, and I looked at them last night. Lennon left the Indian Army very suddenly. That was strange. He was in the Indian Army for eight and a half years. Usually soldiers are in the army for regular times ... five years, or seven years or ten years. So I sent a telegram to some friends in London. The army discovered that he was investigating hypnotic drugs, and they threw him out.'

'But how did you know where the little bottle was, Holmes?' I asked.

'Elementary, my dear Watson. While you were looking after Mr Crane, I was watching Lennon. He kept putting his hand to his left-hand jacket pocket.'

# Appendix: Cricket

Cricket is most popular as a sport in England and Wales, India, Pakistan, Sri Lanka, Bangladesh, South Africa, Zimbabwe, the West Indies (Jamaica, Trinidad, Guyana, Barbados, etc.), Australia and New Zealand. There are teams in more than one hundred countries. In England, it's a summer sport. In India and Pakistan it's the most popular sport of all. Like baseball, cricket is a 'bat and ball' game. There are records of games like cricket in England in 1300. The first international match was England against Australia in 1876.

In cricket, there are two teams. Each team has eleven players. The **batting** team has two **batsmen**. They stand in front of the two **wickets**, and their job is to hit the ball before it hits the wicket. The wickets are twenty-two yards (about twenty metres) away from each other.

The **fielding** team has all eleven of its players on the field. The **bowler** is part of the fielding side. The bowler **bowls** the ball towards the wicket and the batsman tries to hit it. If the batsman misses it, and the ball hits the wicket, the batsman is **out**. He leaves the field and another batsman comes onto the field.

If the batsman hits it, the two batsmen can run between the two wickets. Every time they pass each other in the middle, their team scores one **run**.

If any of the fielding side catches the ball in the air, or if they can throw it back and hit the wicket while the batsmen are in the middle, one batsman is out.

The game continues until ten batsmen are out. This is called an **innings**. Then the other team has an innings. There are two **umpires** (or referees). One has to watch the batsman, the other watches the bowler.

The **wicketkeeper** is part of the fielding side. The wicketkeeper is behind the wicket and tries to catch the ball if the batsman misses.

Cricket is perhaps still more popular among men, but women play it too. We still say 'batsman' for women's cricket.

# Glossary

These extra words are not in the 1,250 words for Level 4. See also the Appendix on cricket for special vocabulary.

**army** a big group of soldiers (the **Indian Army** was the army in India between 1858 and 1947, when India was part of the British Empire; it had British and Indian soldiers)

**bat** (*n, v*) you use a bat to hit a ball in sports like baseball and cricket

**batsman / batsmen** a batsman is the person holding the bat in a game of cricket or baseball

**bowl, bowler** a bowler 'throws' the ball in a special way in a cricket match; this is called *bowling* (see Appendix)

**captain** the leader of a group of people: *the captain of a sports team*; captain is also an officer in an army

**carriage** a carriage has wheels; a horse (or several horses) pull a carriage; also a railway train has several carriages

**case** a problem or mystery that detectives / police officers must find an answer to

**coincidence** when two or more things happen at the same place and at the same time by accident, or by luck

**colonel** an officer in the army; a colonel is below a general but above a captain

**congratulate** when you say to somebody that you are pleased about something they have done, or on a special occasion: *Congratulations! You were first in the sports race / Congratulations on your 21st birthday*

**cough** when air comes out of your chest and throat with a sudden loud noise

**cricket** a popular sport in many countries (see Appendix)

**curry** a hot-tasting Indian food, with chilli and other spices

**disturb** to stop somebody doing something: *She was watching TV, and a phone call disturbed her*

**drug** a type of medicine; medical drugs make you better when you are ill; other drugs (which are illegal) make you behave in a different way

**elementary** easy; the opposite of *difficult*

**expect** think that something is going to happen: *I expect it'll rain later*

**fellow** a man (informal)

**footstep** the sound that a foot makes when it touches the ground; the mark a foot makes on soft ground

**forehead** the front part of your head, above your eyes and nose

**housekeeper** a person you pay to look after your house; they clean, cook, and do other jobs

**hypnotic** (*adj*) something that makes someone hypnotised

**hypnotise** (*v*) to put someone in a state like being asleep; when someone is hypnotised they may obey suggestions which are made to them

**injure** hurt: *He injured his leg during the football match*

**investigate** to find more information about something, especially a crime or a mystery

**landlady** a woman who owns a house, apartment or small hotel, and rents it to people; also **landlord** for men

**limp** walk with some difficulty because you have hurt your leg, knee or foot

**miles an hour** 90 miles an hour is 145 k/h; 50 miles an hour is 80 k/h

**modest** a modest person never talks about the good or clever things that they have done

**nephew** the son of your sister or brother

**patient** a sick person who a doctor is looking after / helping

**pavilion** a building, often used for entertainment or for sport; in Britain, often a building where sportspeople change clothes (see illustration on page 29)

**platform** the place inside a railway station where you stand while you're waiting for a train; the place you stand on when you leave a train

**records** written notes about things that have happened in the past

**rugby football** a sport with fifteen or thirteen players; the ball is the shape of an egg (oval) and players can catch it and carry it in their hands

**score(d)** to get a point (or goal) in a sport

**strike, struck** to hit sharply; **struck** is the past tense

**suntanned** the skin is darker because of the sun

**telegram** in the past, a message sent quickly by telephone, and written at the receiving end

**telegraph pole** a tall piece of wood or metal which carries telephone lines

**tragic** very, very sad

**umpire** referee

**violin** classical musical instrument with four strings

**widow** a woman whose husband has died

**yard** a little less than a metre (92 cm)

# Activities

**1 Look at the story again and find this information. How fast can you find it?**

1 The year in which this story happens.

2 Sherlock Holmes's address.

3 The name of Giles's widow.

4 The time of the train to Devon.

5 The distance between telegraph poles on the Great Western Railway.

6 The type of meat in the curry at Colonel Abbot's house.

7 The things Herbert Crane's farm produced.

8 The number of runs the Havelock team scored.

9 The number of years Dr Lennon was in the Indian Army.

10 The colour of the glass bottle in his pocket.


**2 Mark these sentences true (✓), false (✗) or don't know (?). Correct the false ones.**

1 ☐ Dr Watson hates fresh air.

2 ☐ Colonel Abbot left the army two years earlier.

3 ☐ Giles Pendryth died three hours after the ball hit him.

4 ☐ Both dead players were hit on the forehead.

5 ☐ Colonel Abbot was Giles Pendryth's uncle.

6 ☐ Watson had last played cricket in June.

7 ☐ Watson played well and scored 107.

8 ☐ Colonel Abbot was not really feeling ill.

9 ☐ The ball hit Crane's arm and broke it.

10 ☐ Dr Watson had written a book about hypnotism.

## 3 Complete the sentences with words from the glossary.

1 The smoke from Holmes's pipe made Dr Watson _____.

2 Mrs Hudson was Sherlock Holmes's _____.

3 The train to Devon left from _____ Four.

4 They travelled from Havelock Station to Colonel Abbot's house in a _____.

5 Both Dr Watson and Dr Lennon were in the _____ in India.

6 The hypnotic _____ was in Dr Lennon's pocket.

7 The son of your sister or brother is your _____.

8 Colonel Abbot sent a _____ to Holmes. He was asking for help.

9 While Dr Watson was in Devon, Dr Harris looked after his _____.

10 Lennon _____ Crane in the changing room in the pavilion.

11 Holmes replaced Colonel Abbot and was the _____ for the second innings.

12 Colonel Abbot got his _____ powder from Dr Lennon.

13 The cricket ball _____ the men on their foreheads.

14 Dr Lennon was the _____ of the village cricket team.

15 Juliet became a _____ after Giles's death.

**4 Do these comprehension tasks for chapters 1 to 3.**

    1  When did Holmes usually play the violin?

    2  Why does Dr Watson limp when he walks?

    3  Which sport does Dr Watson prefer?

    4  How many people had been killed in cricket matches during the last twenty-five years?

    5  Does the bowler throw the ball at the batsman?

    6  Why had Holmes already bought the train tickets?

    7  Why was Watson late for the train?

    8  What had he had for breakfast?

    9  How did Holmes know that?

   10  What did Colonel Abbot look like?

   11  How did Giles die?

   12  Why was Giles worried?

   13  Why did Giles refuse to sell his farm?

   14  Where was Juliet when Giles was killed?

   15  What do you know about James Dodds?

**5 Do these comprehension tasks for chapters 4 to 6.**

    1  Where does the curry powder come from?

    2  Why did Dr Lennon come to Colonel Abbot's house?

    3  Why can't Dr Watson run fast?

    4  When was the last time Dr Watson played cricket?

    5  Who was the best player in the Havelock team?

6   What did Dr Watson do after breakfast?

7   Where did Holmes go? Why?

8   Was Colonel Abbot telling the truth about his heart problem?

9   Where was Herbert Crane while they were having tea?

10   Where did the flash of light come from?

11   What did Crane do when he saw the flash?

12   What happened to him?

13   How had Dr Lennon hypnotised Crane?

14   What was the railway company going to do?

15   How did Holmes know where the bottle was?

## 6   Find examples in the story where ...

1   Sherlock Holmes was not telling the truth.

2   Dr Watson was talking about himself.

## 7   Find information on the Internet.

1   When was *The Sign of the Four* written?

2   Name two actors who have played Sherlock Holmes in films.

3   Find the titles of the collections of Sherlock Holmes short stories by Conan Doyle.

4   Who played Dr Watson in the 2010 TV series?

5   What is the title of the 2011 Sherlock Holmes film?

**Sherlock Holmes and Doctor Watson** are detectives who appeared in books by Arthur Conan Doyle (1859–1930). Conan Doyle was a doctor of medicine and a writer. He wrote four novels and fifty-six short stories about Holmes between 1887 and 1927.

There have been more than two hundred Sherlock Holmes films, many TV and radio plays, books by other writers, short stories and computer games about Sherlock Holmes.

*The Case of the Dead Batsman* is one of the many new stories about Sherlock Holmes and Dr Watson. It was not written by Arthur Conan Doyle.

### A Sherlock Holmes joke

Sherlock Holmes and Dr Watson were on holiday. They were camping in the country. They put up their tent, went inside, and went to sleep. At three o'clock in the morning, Holmes woke Watson.

'Watson! Watson!' he said. 'Wake up!'

'Is it morning already?' said Watson.

'No, no,' said Holmes. 'Watson, tell me what you can see.'

Watson looked up. 'I can see the stars,' he said.

'So, you're a detective. What does that tell you?'

Watson thought for a moment. 'Well, it tells me that it's a beautiful clear night.'

'Anything else?' asked Holmes.

'Er, yes. I'm looking at the North Star and at the moon, and I can see that it is about three o'clock in the morning.'

'Yes, yes,' said Holmes. 'Is that all?'

'Yes, that's all. What should it tell me?'

'Watson, you fool. It should tell you that someone has stolen our tent!'

# Other titles available in the series

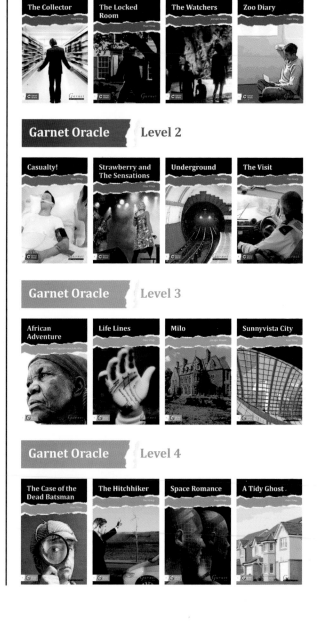

**Garnet Oracle** — Level 1

- The Collector
- The Locked Room
- The Watchers
- Zoo Diary

**Garnet Oracle** — Level 2

- Casualty!
- Strawberry and The Sensations
- Underground
- The Visit

**Garnet Oracle** — Level 3

- African Adventure
- Life Lines
- Milo
- Sunnyvista City

**Garnet Oracle** — Level 4

- The Case of the Dead Batsman
- The Hitchhiker
- Space Romance
- A Tidy Ghost